# SPORTS GREAT CHARLES BARKLEY

# —Sports Great Books—

# SPORTS GREAT
# CHARLES
# BARKLEY

Glen Macnow

*—Sports Great Books—*

**ENSLOW PUBLISHERS, INC.**

| | |
|---|---|
| 44 Fadem Road | P.O. Box 38 |
| Box 699 | Aldershot |
| Springfield, N.J. 07081 | Hants GU12 6BP |
| U.S.A. | U.K. |

*Dedicated to my wife, Judy, who makes it all worthwhile.*

**Library of Congress Cataloging-in-Publication Data**

Macnow, Glen
    Sports great Charles Barkley /Glen Macnow
        p. cm. — (Sports great books)
    Includes index.
    Summary: Follows the life and career of the powerful forward drafted by the
Philadelphia 76ers in 1984.
    ISBN 0-89490-386-1
    1. Barkley, Charles, 1963– —Juvenile literature. 2. Basketball players—United
States—Biography—Juvenile literature. 3. Philadelphia 76ers (Basketball
team)—Juvenile literature. [1. Barkley, Charles, 1963– . 2. Basketball players. 3.
Afro-Americans—Biography.] I. Title. II. Series.
GV884.B28M33 1992
796.323'092—dc20
[B]
                                                        91-45827
                                                           CIP
                                                            AC

Printed in the United States of America

10 9 8 7 6

**Photo Credits:** Auburn University, p. 20; Andrew D. Bernstein, p. 51; Nancy R.
Cunningham/Philadelphia 76ers, p. 36; Zack Hill/Philadelphia 76ers, pp. 29, 45,
50; Ed Mahan/Philadelphia 76ers, p. 42; Mike Maicher/Philadelphia 76ers, pp. 10,
12, 14, 17, 22, 25, 28, 31, 40, 55, 57, 59; Philadelphia 76ers, pp. 8, 33, 38, 48.

**Cover Photo:** AP/Wide World Photos

# Contents

# *Acknowledgments*

Thanks to Zachary Hill of the Phildelphia 76ers for his help in providing information and photographs. Thanks also to James Cohen of ESPN for his research help and guidance.

# *Chapter 1*

The National Basketball Association's best players gathered in Charlotte, North Carolina for the 1991 All-Star game. Michael Jordan was there to represent the Eastern Conference, along with stars like Patrick Ewing and Joe Dumars. Magic Johnson led the Western Conference team, which included giants David Robinson and Hakeem Olajuwon.

Also on the Eastern Conference team was Charles Barkley. Everyone agreed that Barkley deserved to be an all-star. The Philadelphia 76ers' star forward was—as usual—averaging close to 30 points and 11 rebounds a game during the season.

But many fans and players thought that Barkley should not play in the All-Star game. For weeks he had been suffering from a broken bone in his left foot. The injury made it painful for Barkley to run and even more painful for him to jump. "My wife thinks I should take a few days to rest during the All- Star break," Barkley said. "And I suppose she's right. The important thing is to be healthy for the 76ers."

Charles is one of professional basketball's most entertaining players.

The men who run the NBA, however, told Barkley he must play. They wanted him in Charlotte because, like Johnson and Jordan, he is a "marquee player," one whose skills can excite the crowd. After all, they said, no one in the league plays with a style like Barkley's. He is built like a truck but moves like a sports car. And his dunks are the most thunderous in basketball.

So Barkley came to the game. Most people expected him to play a few minutes and then watch the other all-stars go at it while he rested his injured foot.

It didn't work out that way. Before the game started, Barkley told his fellow all-stars that—bad foot and all—he planned to nab every rebound. Some of the players laughed at that boast. But Hersey Hawkins, Barkley's teammate on the 76ers, knew better. Hawkins knew that when Barkley said something like that, he had a way of backing it up.

When the All-Star game ended, Charles Barkley had led the East to a 116–114 win over the West. He walked off the court—or limped off the court—with the most valuable player award.

Among all the NBA's top stars that night, Barkley shined the brightest. He scored 17 points and grabbed a whopping 22 rebounds. No one had gotten as many rebounds in an All-Star game since Wilt Chamberlain in 1967. Barkley also had four assists and a blocked shot. He accomplished so much that some players joked they also saw him selling tickets to the game and parking cars in the lot outside the arena.

"I hate Charles," joked Magic Johnson of the losing West afterwards. "He really controlled the game. I guarded him at one point, and I thought I had him boxed out. All of a sudden, he had me boxed out. I now realize how big and strong he is."

The All-Star game was tied midway through the second quarter. Then Barkley took over. First, he bravely stuffed a shot by 270-pounder Kevin Duckworth. He picked up the ball and fired a perfect bounce pass to Hawkins for a lay up. When the West came down the floor again, Barkley outfought three seven-footers for the rebound. He dribbled the length of the floor, bulling through everyone in his path. He looked to pass the ball, but none of his teammates had caught up with him. So he threw down a one-handed tomahawk jam that brought the arena crowd to its feet. Soon, the fans started chanting his name.

In the space of five minutes, Barkley had six rebounds and seven points. He used his strength to turn the game into a

Barkley meets basketball legend Wilt Chamberlain, the only man to grab as many rebounds in an NBA All-Star game as Charles Barkley.

freeway pileup. When the first half ended, the East had the lead—and never gave it up.

In the locker room after the game, reporters asked Barkley how he could play so well with a broken bone. But Barkley would not answer. "I don't want to talk about my foot anymore," he said. "My foot is going to hurt, but I'm going to play. I have too much desire to help my team."

Desire? No one could ever doubt Charles Barkley's desire. He is neither the tallest player in the NBA nor the fastest—but he is one of the best. He does not possess Larry Bird's soft shot, nor Magic Johnson's lightning-quick moves, nor Michael Jordan's ability to fly. Still, he is a star among stars. The main reason is his thirst for success.

"With Charles on the floor, you figure something is going to happen and that, nine times out of ten, it's going to be something good for his team," said Chris Ford, coach of the 76ers' chief rival, the Boston Celtics. Ford compared Barkley with his own superstar, forward Larry Bird. Both men play as if they are on a mission. Both hate to lose. Both are driven to always do their best.

From an early age, Charles Wade Barkley was determined to do his best. He practiced harder than the players around him and carefully studied the game even when he wasn't playing. When he ran up against an obstacle, he did not give up. Instead, he tried twice as hard and worked until he was able to accomplish his goal.

For instance, when Charles was fifteen, he was told that he was too short and too fat to play on the high school basketball team. The coach said that Charles could not jump high enough to be a good player.

When Charles heard that, he decided that maybe he couldn't teach himself to grow, but he could teach himself to jump. He spent hours every day hopping over a fence in his

Charles likes to play right under the basket, where the roughest action takes place.

backyard in Leeds, Alabama. The jumping helped him lose weight and become more athletic. Soon, he made the team. After a while, he became a starter. Finally, he won a scholarship to Auburn University.

Years later, Barkley was again told that he was too short. His style of play in college was to crash the boards, to stand near the basket and dare opponents to push out his 300-pound body. He is built a lot like a refrigerator—and it's very difficult to move a refrigerator.

Upon entering the National Basketball Association in 1984, many experts thought Barkley was not tall enough to play under the basket. He stands just under six-feet-five inches tall. Meanwhile, the average player in the NBA is six-feet-nine, and every team has two or three players who stand taller than seven feet. These giants usually control the play of the game, stuffing the basketball and grabbing the rebounds off the backboards.

Barkley, the experts said, would have to change his style of play. It was believed that a man his size could never be a good inside player in the pros.

The experts were wrong. In the 1986-87 season, Barkley became the shortest player in the forty-five-year history of the NBA to lead the league in rebounds. What Barkley doesn't have in height, he makes up for in desire. And that desire helps him jump higher than the giants around him.

Matt Goukas, a former coach of the 76ers, said that when Barkley is standing still, he does not look like the kind of player who can be a force in basketball. But when Barkley starts to move, Goukas said, he can do remarkable things. And when Barkley speaks, you begin to understand that his heart is what makes him so great. He just wants to succeed more than the other players.

Barkley is not a tall player, but he outhustles his opponents.

Being the top rebounder is not Barkley's only accomplishment. Six times in his first seven seasons, he averaged more than 20 points a game. He has played in five All-Star games. His exciting style of play has been described as being like a bottle of soda pop that someone shakes until it explodes all over the court.

"My momma told me long ago to let my emotions out," Barkley once said. "And she told me always to try my best. I've lived by those rules my whole life. If you don't try your best, what's the point of trying at all?"

# *Chapter 2*

In the broiling summertime heat of Leeds, Alabama, a fifteen-year-old boy spent hours every day challenging a chain-link fence. The determined teenager would run at the four-foot-high fence and try to leap over it. Sometimes he didn't make it, skinning his knees or banging his elbows. His mother said he looked like someone who had gotten in a car crash. But he practiced and practiced for months. Finally, he was able to stand next to the fence and hop over it flat-footed.

The boy was Charles Wade Barkley, then known as Wade to his friends. At that time, the summer before his junior year of high school, he stood 5 feet 10 inches tall. The high school basketball coach, Billy Coupland, had told Wade that if he didn't grow, his chances of making the team were not good. Wade desperately wanted to make the team. So he decided he would just have to learn to outjump the taller boys.

He spent hours every day hopping back and forth over that backyard fence. He taught himself to jump, and at the same time he did begin to grow. By the winter, he had sprouted to

As a boy, Charles practice jumping every day. Now he can dunk the ball with ease.

six-feet-two and won a starting position on the Leeds High School team.

Charles was born in Leeds on February 20, 1963. His parents were divorced when he was a baby. His father moved away to California and stopped seeing Charles. A few years later, Charles's mom, Charcey, married a man named Clee Glenn and had two other sons. When Charles was eleven, Mr. Glenn was killed in a car crash. So Charles lost two fathers as a child, which is tough for any kid to handle.

Charles's grandparents, Adolphus and Johnnie Edwards, helped raise him. And today, Charles's most special relationship is with his grandmother. She gives him advice on everything from raising his own daughter to dealing with NBA referees to handling the responsibilities of being a celebrity.

Barkley's mother recalls that her son was so determined to become a star that, as a teenager, he didn't have time for anything else but running, practicing and playing basketball. "He would run for hours in the hot sun," Mrs. Glenn said. "And he'd jump and jump over that fence. I'd watch him fall down and hurt himself, and I would want him to stop. But he told me, 'Momma, I'm going to play in the NBA.' And he meant it. Nothing was going to stop him."

Charles and his mother believed in his dream—even if no one else did. But most of the time, Barkley was only an average high school player. His leaping skills made him great at blocking shots and grabbing rebounds. His own shots, however, were often off target, and he had trouble dribbling and passing the ball to teammates.

In his junior year, Charles was just the third- or fourth-best player on the Leeds High team, said the coach. He averaged 13 points and 11 rebounds a game. Leeds won 25 games while losing just 7.

Barkley grew to six-feet-four as a high school senior. And his hours of practice began to pay off. He started grabbing offensive rebounds and jamming them through the hoop in one motion. One night he pulled down 30 rebounds in a game against rival Ensley High. Overall, he averaged 19 points and 18 rebounds a game.

Leeds went 26-3 and was invited to play in a Christmas tournament in Tuscaloosa, Alabama. Dozens of coaches and scouts came to the tournament to watch Bobby Lee Hurt, a tall center who was regarded as the best high school player in the state. But when Hurt came up against Barkley, the state suddenly had a new best player.

Barkley had 25 points and 20 rebounds in a game against Hurt, leading Leeds High to victory. He blocked several of Hurt's shots and held the taller player to 20 points and just 9 rebounds. Now the scouts were excited about this new player, the chubby forward from Leeds who could jump to the sky.

Colleges from around the South started to offer scholarships. Barkley chose Auburn University because it was near his home. He wasn't ready to leave his family, telling friends that he was "still a baby." What he meant was that he was seventeen years old, but he was not prepared for living away from the people he loved.

That was OK with Charles's mom. Charcey Glenn worked hard cleaning houses when Charles was growing up. Her son helped by taking care of their house—washing, cooking, ironing the clothes. He even changed all the bedsheets twice a week. He wanted to make life easier for his mother and often promised her that he would one day become rich playing basketball and buy her everything she wanted. She never tried to talk him out of his goal.

But first, Charles had to deal with the pressures of college. At Auburn University, the basketball coach was Sonny Smith.

He was the toughest coach for whom Barkley ever played. Smith demanded hard work and top results from his players. Anyone who failed to follow Smith's rules faced strong punishment—as Charles would soon find out.

From the start, Barkley and Smith did not get along. Charles had grown to just under six-feet-five, but his weight had grown even more. He had entered college at 260 pounds, but he liked the food so much that his weight quickly grew to 300 pounds. Fans and opponents found Barkley's shape something to laugh at. They gave him nicknames like "Boy Gorge," and "The Round Mound of Rebound" and "Bread Truck." In some arenas, fans threw empty pizza boxes from the seats to make fun of his eating habits. One time, as a joke, someone had a meal delivered to Barkley on the Auburn bench.

Coach Smith found none of these things funny. He felt that Barkley's weight slowed him down and caused him to lose energy. The coach tried to make Barkley work harder at

Charles during his years at Auburn University.

practice, but Barkley wanted to push himself only in games that really counted. Smith told Barkley to lay off the snacks and go to class. Barkley did neither.

During practice one day, Smith screamed at Barkley to "do something." So the next time down the court, Barkley jammed in a rebound so hard that it snapped the rim from the backboard. Another time, Smith had Barkley run "gut-churner" drills with the Auburn football team. Players had to run up and down stadium steps until they quit or threw up. Barkley did neither, but he kept running.

In another try to make Barkley lose weight, Smith had him run with heavy cinder blocks on his back. He made Barkley run laps around the gym and roll 50 yards, back and forth, on the football field. Once, Smith made Barkley run a mile with a bucket of water in each hand.

The plan didn't work. Barkley kept gaining weight. But he also kept improving as a player. In one memorable game against the tough Georgetown Hoyas Barkley did the impossible. He blocked a shot by Georgetown center Patrick Ewing, who stood seven inches taller than Charles. In that contest, Charles scored 24 points and snared 16 rebounds. His performance wasn't enough, however, as Georgetown won.

In three seasons at Auburn, Barkley averaged 14.1 points and 9.6 rebounds a game. As a junior in 1984, he was the Southeastern Conference Player of the Year and helped the Tigers to their first NCAA tournament berth. The "Round Mound," extra weight and all, became a national sensation. Here was a chunky kid who set shot-blocking and rebounding records and developed such a soft shooting touch that he made 64 percent of his shots over his college career.

A few years later, Coach Smith admitted that he had been too hard on Barkley. Smith said that Charles was not used to discipline, and did not like it. Still, the coach felt that some of

Barkley has been known to jam the ball so hard that it breaks the backboard.

his toughness had helped Barkley. It taught Charles how to push himself to be as great as he wanted to be.

The summer after his junior year, Charles went on a diet. He slimmed down to a muscular dynamo of 265 pounds who could thunder through opponents. And he began to think about another important decision. After his great college season, Barkley knew he could leave Auburn and become a first-round pick in the pro basketball draft. His family needed the money he would earn, and it would be a chance to realize a lifelong dream. Besides, his relationship with Coach Smith did not seem likely to improve.

But he also wanted to remain in college and work toward earning his degree. Everyone at Auburn and basketball fans from around Alabama were hoping he would stay. They felt the school could become a national champion if Barkley was there to lead the team.

Barkley was torn. In the end, he decided that the chance to go pro and be drafted early was too good to pass up. So he applied for the NBA June draft. As the day neared, Barkley wondered which team would select him.

The 1984 NBA draft will always be remembered as one of the best in the league's history. Hakeem Olajuwon, the giant center from Nigeria, was picked first by the Houston Rockets. Michael Jordan soon followed, going to the Chicago Bulls. Other fine players coming out of that draft included Sam Perkins, Alvin Robertson, and John Stockton.

The Philadelphia 76ers had the fifth pick in that year's draft. Their choice: Auburn forward Charles Barkley.

# Chapter 3

Barkley was thrilled to go to Philadelphia. Back then, the 76ers, the Boston Celtics, and the Los Angeles Lakers were regarded as the best teams in the league.

Before that afternoon in June, Charles had expected to go to a weak team. In the NBA, the teams that lose the most games get the first draft picks after the season. That means that most great college players get chosen by bad teams. They must learn to play pro ball in a losing atmosphere. But the 76ers had made a trade the season before to get the first-round pick of the Los Angeles Clippers. That turned out to be the fifth pick overall—and they were able to get Barkley.

Barkley knew he was lucky to go to a good team. He knew that no one expected him to become the team's top player right away. When the Sixers lost, he wouldn't be blamed. And when they won, he could share in the fun. Mostly, he planned to learn by watching his talented teammates.

Certainly, the 76ers were a team full of stars during Barkley's rookie season. Julius Erving, better known as "Dr. J.," started at one forward spot. Erving's high-flying style and

As a rookie, Charles (34) got to play with the great center Moses Malone (2).

slam dunks made him the most exciting player in basketball. The center was Moses Malone, a mountain-sized man who led the NBA in rebounding six different seasons. Sharpshooter Andrew Toney started at one guard spot. Reliable Maurice Cheeks started at the other. The other forward was Bobby Jones, a defensive wizard who was nearing the end of a solid twelve-year pro career.

Into this mix came Barkley. The 76ers' thinking was simple: They wanted a good rebounder who could help Malone under the basket. And they wanted an exciting player who could come off the bench to replace Jones midway through the game and score some points. Barkley seemed perfect for both jobs.

The Sixers were excited about having Barkley wear their red-and-blue uniform. And Barkley was just as excited. Sixers' assistant coach Jack McMahon predicted Barkley would become a great player. "He has very fast feet, he can jump, and he knows how to rebound," McMahon said. "Besides, given his shape and size, who's going to match up with him?"

At the club's rookie camp in Princeton, New Jersey, McMahon was waiting for Barkley with a little test. He would create tricky rebound tries and count how many a player could come away with.

McMahon had tried the same test a few years earlier with Darryl Dawkins. That former Sixer had the talent but lacked the drive it takes to turn a good player into a great one. Usually, Dawkins was able to pull down about 5 rebounds for every 20 tries.

But when McMahon tried the test on Barkley, the new player was able to grab 12 or 13 of every 20 tries. The test, McMahon said, really showed how hard a man was willing to work. And who worked harder than Barkley?

When the 1984-85 season began, Barkley quickly learned that he was as talented as the NBA's top veterans. That part of the job wasn't as hard as he expected. Instead, the toughest part of being a pro was getting used to life away from his family. Because he left school a year early, Barkley—at twenty-one—was a year younger than most rookies in the NBA. Besides, life on the road in the NBA is different from life with a college team. Pro teams play 82 games a season. College teams play about 30. And pro players have no coaches or teachers to "baby-sit" for them. They have to make their own decisions and take care of themselves. Barkley rented an apartment in downtown Philadelphia. Still, he called his mother almost every day to ask her advice.

Asked early in his rookie season how he liked the NBA, Barkley told a reporter that it was OK, but certainly not as nice as Leeds, Alabama. There's no place like home, he said.

Around teammates, however, Barkley never let on that he was homesick or nervous about being a newcomer. While waiting for his luggage at an airport one day, Barkley got angry when an older player called him "Rook," a nickname for "Rookie."

"Don't call me Rook," Barkley snarled at his teammate. "I told you I ain't no rookie." Of course, he was a rookie. He just didn't play or act like one.

Mostly, though, he had a good time with his teammates. His closest friend was Julius Erving, who had already played thirteen years as a pro. The great Dr. J. saw Barkley as a player in his own mold. Comparing the way Barkley played as a first-year player to the way he played, Erving said, "He is a thoroughbred. He just needs to be given some sneakers and pointed in the right direction. He'll make the rest happen. Charles has one quality that I think is very important. He

The biggest influence on Barkley's career was Julius Erving—the great Dr. J.

doesn't want to be just a good player in this league. He wants to be a star in this league."

So Erving took the young rookie aside at least once a week that season for private lessons. The teaching included topics such as how to use the head fake and when to take a foul. And it went beyond that. Erving taught Barkley how to lead life as a pro. He taught the rookie how to stay in shape and stay out of trouble. And he explained what duties go along with great talent. A star player, Erving said, must always know how to behave himself on—and off—the court.

Erving told everyone that when he retired, Charles would be the player who would provide the thrills to make people jump out of their seats every once in a while. He predicted that

Charles's exciting style makes him a favorite with 76ers fans

the Philadelphia fans would love Barkley's enthusiasm and emotion.

In fact, Barkley became a fan favorite within weeks of joining the 76ers. The club, although talented, was getting older and playing without much zip. Barkley, however, played with the joy of a little boy. He never stopped running, diving after loose balls, and shouting at players on other teams. Sometimes, he acted more like a football player than a basketball player. The 76ers' fans cheered his every move.

For the season, Barkley averaged 14 points a game, even though he was just a part-time player. He helped out Malone by snaring nearly nine rebounds per game. Best of all, he made the 76ers more fun to watch.

"When Charles is in there, our whole team picks up," said Billy Cunningham, who was Philadelphia's coach during Barkley's rookie season. "He's like adding a lit match to a few sticks of dynamite."

Cunningham saw his prize rookie as a rare player who can play with—and without—the basketball almost as if he were alone on the practice court. Few players have such talent—Erving, Magic Johnson of the Lakers, Larry Bird of the Celtics. They can rebound, pass, dribble, shoot, and play defense as if each basket might win the game. To Cunningham, Barkley could join that group of great players if he worked hard enough.

Still, Barkley made some rookie mistakes. One was his habit of sometimes daydreaming during the game. Another was Barkley's defense. He had never been a great defensive player. Even today he admits that guarding the other team's players is his least-favorite part of the game. Barkley insists that he can play tough defense when he has to. He just doesn't like to.

Nothing, and no one, can stop Barkley when he decides to drive for the basket.

In one game against the Detroit Pistons during his first season, Barkley forgot to cover the Pistons' center, Bill Laimbeer. That allowed Laimbeer to score a few easy baskets. "Help, Charles! Help!" Coach Cunningham shouted. "Get your mind in the game!" Barkley bowed his head like a student caught napping in class, but he quickly woke up. He grabbed the next rebound, dribbled past three opponents, and slam-dunked the basketball. The Philadelphia fans went nuts.

In the 1985 playoffs, Barkley's mind never wandered. During the Sixers' thirteen playoff games, he grew from being a good rookie into a great one. He had the most rebounds on his team in ten of those thirteen games. He averaged 15 points a game.

In one opening-round game against the Milwaukee Bucks, Barkley scored 19 points, had 7 rebounds, and 5 blocked shots. He led a second-quarter 76ers' comeback by sinking two three-point shots. He helped stop the Bucks down the stretch with two steals of the ball. And when Bucks' forward Paul Mokeski tried to surprise the 76ers by driving right down the lane toward the basket, Charles whacked him on the head and sent him rolling. It earned Barkley a foul, but it also scared Mokeski so much that he never again wandered close to the Philadelphia basket. Late in the game, Barkley hobbled off on a sprained left ankle. But he had already led his team to a 109-104 win.

"Charles saved our bacon tonight," Sixers' general manager Pat Williams said after the game. "I can't remember the last time a rookie did this well in the playoffs."

After beating the Bucks and the Washington Bullets, the 76ers lost to the Boston Celtics in the Eastern Conference finals. For Barkley, it had been a great rookie year. When it ended, he went back to Alabama to spend the off-season relaxing. He hoped people would ask him about Julius

Barkley battles for a rebound against Bernard King of the Washington Bullets.

Erving—just so he had the chance to talk about how exciting it was to learn from Dr. J.

But Erving, the teacher, had just one more lesson for his star student. He warned Charles to stay in shape during the off-season. If Barkley failed to work out, if he gained back all the weight he had worked so hard to lose, Erving said he would quickly find himself out of the NBA.

Barkley promised to listen.

# *Chapter 4*

When Barkley went home after his rookie season, he kept Dr. J.'s advice in mind. He worked out all summer and cut his dinner portions back from three entire pizzas to just one. He lost about ten pounds of fat. At the same time, he gained muscle and energy. The Round Mound of Rebound was no more.

At the start of the 1985-86 season, Sixer's trainer Pat Croce decided to test Barkley's strength. Croce had the player try lifing a 200-pound weight. Charles played with it as if it were a toy. Then Croce had Charles push against him with his legs. Charles nearly broke the trainer in half. Barkley's strength, Croce said, had become unbelievable—even scary.

Because of Barkley's great performance in the playoffs the year before, the Sixers gave him a much larger role in his second season. Erving was moved from forward to guard, giving Barkley more room to work under the other team's basket. And Moses Malone was moved outside a few feet, giving Charles a chance to grab more rebounds.

The 1985–86 Philadelphia 76ers huddle up.

The plan worked. Barkley averaged exactly 20 points per game in 1985-86. He finished second in the NBA in rebounding, behind only Bill Laimbeer of the Detroit Pistons. By the end of the season, the team that had belonged to Dr. J. on the court now belonged to Barkley. It was as if the student had become the teacher. At just twenty-three years of age, he was the top star.

"We have seen the future and he wears No. 34," Sixers' general manager Pat Williams told a national TV audience at the end of the season. "Charles might be the most gifted athlete in America. Can you think of anyone else with that size, that speed, that agility? Charles is in charge."

Charles had to be even more in charge the next season. Sixers' coaches decided that Malone, a slow player, kept Barkley from running his fastest on the court. So before the 1986-87 season, they traded Malone to the Washington Bullets. The trade was not a good one, however. The player that Philadelphia got in return, center Jeff Ruland, injured his knee and played just five games for the 76ers.

Andrew Toney, the 76ers' sharp-shooting guard also got injured and stopped playing. Veteran forward Bobby Jones retired.

Most importantly, Erving was thirty-six years old and losing speed. Early in the 1986-87 season, he announced that it would be his last. Barkley, he said, would have to take over. It was a lot of responsibility, Erving told reporters, but Charles had broad shoulders. There was no doubt that he could handle it. The team, Dr. J. said, could now be nicknamed "Barkley's Bunch."

Barkley enjoyed becoming a team leader. But he was also frustrated. When he joined the pros, his teammates included some of the greatest players in NBA history. Now most of those men were gone. The young players who replaced them were not nearly as talented.

The changes showed on the court. The Sixers fell from 58 wins in Charles's rookie year to 54 wins in 1985-86, and then to 45 wins in 1986-87. The next year they won just 36 of the 82 regular season games. They failed to make the NBA playoffs for the first time in thirteen seasons.

Barkley did not enjoy playing for a losing team. His teammates now were mostly average players. He missed the stars he had come up with. Moses Malone, Julius Erving, Bobby Jones, Andrew Toney, and Maurice Cheeks helped make the 76ers one of the greatest teams ever. Now, only Cheeks was left to help Barkley.

Certainly no one could blame Barkley for the 76ers' tumble. Even as the team got worse, he kept getting better. His scoring average rose in each of his first four seasons, up to

A serious injury to guard Andrew Toney hurt the 76ers' chances in the 1986–87 season.

28.3 points per game in 1987-88. In his third year, he became the shortest player ever to lead the NBA in rebounds. For three straight years, he won the NBA's Schick Pivotal Player Award for all-around greatness. Every player's points, rebounds, assists, and steals were loaded into a computer, which then chose the best in the league. Barkley beat out players like Michael Jordan, Magic Johnson, and Larry Bird—and he did it three years in a row.

Players and coaches around the league now knew how talented Barkley was. They nicknamed him "Sir Charles" and were quick to praise him:

* Cleveland Cavaliers' coach George Karl: "It's dawning on Barkley that he can be the best. He's close enough that he can smell it. And he wants it. You can see it in his eyes."

* Atlanta Hawks' star Dominique Wilkins: "He's unbelievable. He's so big, so strong and so active around the glass that it's impossible to beat him one on one because you're not as strong as he is. Charles is really amazing."

* San Antonio Spurs' general manager Bob Bass: "He honks his horn and everybody gets out of the way. If somebody tries to take a charge with Barkley, I believe it's going to be their last game."

One of the most memorable moments from Barkley's early career was the 1986 playoffs against the Bucks. Moses Malone was injured just before the playoffs, leaving Barkley to face the Bucks' front line by himself. Milwaukee used three seven-footers—Paul Mokeski, Randy Breuer, and Alton Lister—but they could not control Charles. He averaged 15 rebounds and 28 points over the seven-game series. He also played a remarkable 45 minutes per game. The pace finally caught up with him in game seven, when he tired out and the Sixers lost a 113-112 heartbreaker. Barkley worried afterward that he had let his teammates down. All of them knew,

Barkley positions for a rebound against Kenny Gattison of the Charlotte Hornets.

however, that without Charles, they would not even have reached game seven.

Two things make Barkley a special basketball player. The first is his desire. Barkley says he plays hard because he wants to be special. He doesn't want people to say, "Charles is a good player." He wants them to say, "Charles is the best." His pride, he says, is what sets him apart.

Anyone needing proof has only to look at Barkley up close. Ugly scratches crisscross his upper arms and shoulders. They are the result of thousands of battles under the backboard in which players claw for rebounds. Barkley knows that he could move away and get fewer scratches. But he would also get fewer rebounds. The key to his game is hard work. There are guys in the league who are bigger than Barkley. There are guys who have more talent. But nobody outworks him.

The second special thing about Barkley is his style of play. Thousands of men have played in the NBA, but none has ever played exactly like Barkley. Most basketball players are tall and trim and graceful looking. Barkley is none of those things. Sometimes he plays like a rhino, charging straight ahead with his wide body, butting anyone who dares to get in the way. Other times he is as quick as a mousetrap, surprising sleeker opponents by beating them to the ball. He can dribble behind his back, just like a guard. And he can dunk with such force that he can bend the 2,200-pound iron basket supports.

Dunking is what he likes to do best. Remember the little boy who had trouble leaping over his backyard fence? These days he is one of the most feared dunkers in the NBA. Barkley is a strength-dunker who is able to throw the ball down in traffic while helpless defenders cling to his arms. "I'm like winter," Barkley likes to say, "because you know I'm coming and there's nothing you can do to stop me."

Boston Celtics great Kevin McHale knows how hard it is to move Barkley away from the basket.

There are other reasons for his success. Barkley may not look graceful, but Larry Bird said that he has the best body control in the NBA. According to Bird, Barkley and Michael Jordan are the best in the business at driving through the other team to get off a good shot. Bird's long-time Celtics teammate, Kevin McHale, said Barkley's great strength is the key. He said that trying to move Barkley away from a rebound is like trying to push a soda machine across the floor.

To see how many different ways Barkley excels, a fan just has to check the statistics. Through his first seven seasons, Charles has made 58 percent of his shots—a tremendous figure that ranks at the top of the NBA. He has averaged more than 11 rebounds per game. He is always among the league's top five in scoring average. And, for a forward, he gets a lot of steals.

Still, Barkley has his problems on the court. He usually leads Philadelphia in turnovers, which means he makes mistakes that give the ball to the other team. He has been known to take fouls at bad times. In fact, every year he hurts his team by fouling out of five or six games.

Perhaps his biggest flaw—at least from the point of view of NBA officials—is his temper. Charles usually leads the league in technical fouls, which are given by referees to players who argue too much or play too rough. It's not that Charles is trying to complain or hurt his opponents. Instead, it's that he is sometimes unable to control his emotions.

"I see the way other players look at me sometimes like, 'What's with you? What are you trying to prove?'" Barkley said. "Some people think I'm cocky or that I'm a bad guy. But I'm just playing the only way I know how. That's all-out and with my heart."

# Chapter 5

In some ways, Charles Barkley is just like most other athletes.

First, he has beaten great odds to become a professional. Second, he plays his sport to win. Third, his chief goal is to get a championship for his team.

But that's all on the court. Off the court, Charles Barkley is different. Other athletes speak cautiously. They answer reporters' questions by giving safe answers. They talk about "winning one game at a time" or "giving 110 percent." Those answers don't really mean anything and won't stir up trouble.

Charles Barkley is not like that. His answers are never predictable or boring. Instead, they are the truth as he sees it. Charles says whatever is on his mind. Usually, he does not think about what the results might be.

In some ways, this trait makes Charles Barkley a refreshing superstar. Who else would say, "If I was seven feet tall, I would be illegal in three states?" Who else could call Larry Bird "the most obnoxious man I ever played against" and get away with it? Certainly, Charles Barkley is an honest man. His words may be controversial, but they come straight from his heart.

A few times, though, Barkley's mouth and his deeds have gotten him into trouble. He has been known to criticize his teammates and swear at fans. He often argues with the referees.

The NBA commissioner keeps a behavior file on each player in the league. One suspects that Barkley's file takes up a whole drawer. He has been suspended for fighting with opponents, for arguing with fans, and, once, for spitting into the crowd. He has said he was sorry each time. But he also said he has no plans to change his personality.

Charles hosts a weekly radio show in Philadelphia to tell fans about what's on his mind.

Barkley likes to tell people that he is a basketball player—not a politician. In other words, he doesn't have to please the public to win. He just has to do his job. The day that fans in other cities start tossing him flowers, Charles says, is the day he'll know it's time to retire.

The funny thing about it is that, away from the arena, Charles Barkley is one of the nicest men in sports. Just ask new members of the 76ers, who end up staying at his house—nicknamed "Hotel Barkley"—until they can find a place to live. Or ask the sick children whom he visits in hospitals. Or ask anyone who has seen this giant of a man cuddle his baby daughter.

"Many players are really jerks who want people to think they're nice," said Dave Kosky, the former public relations director for the 76ers. "But Charles is a nice guy who wants people to think he's a jerk. It's as if he doesn't want to lose that 'bad-guy' image."

In arenas on the road, Barkley is cast as the villain. He is probably booed more loudly than any other player in the NBA. But he takes the heat and actually seems to enjoy it. In Philadelphia, of course, he is a fan favorite.

Frequently, Charles will play to the balcony like an actor in a play. He raises a clenched fist after a dunk or pats the referee on the rear when he believes the official has made a good call—even if it's against him. During some road games, he'll carry on a running argument with heckling fans from the opening tip-off until the final buzzer. He'll grin at the crowd or stick out his tongue.

That's all in good fun. But a few times it has gone beyond that. Once, in early 1991, Charles lost control of his emotions during a game against the New Jersey Nets at the Meadowlands. A fan sitting courtside kept shouting racial insults at Barkley. Finally, in the fourth quarter, Charles had heard enough. With play stopped for a foul shot, Barkley walked past the screaming man and spit toward him. But he missed his target and hit an eight-year-old girl who was there with her family. Immediately, it seemed, the entire crowd of 15,000 began booing Barkley.

Charles felt terrible. Not only had he done something wrong by trying to spit at the fan, but he had hit a little girl. Afterward, he said he had snapped and admitted it was a stupid thing to do. He called up the girl the next day to apologize. She forgave him. But the NBA was not so forgiving. It fined Barkley $45,000 and suspended him for one game, which the 76ers lost.

When Barkley loses control, it all stems from his tremendous desire to win. He is a passionate player who cannot stand losing and must get the most out of every minute. When he makes a mistake, he grabs his head in despair. When he power dunks over Patrick Ewing, he pumps his fist and jumps for joy.

Barkley said he does these things not to show off, but to get himself pumped up. Besides, he asks, what's wrong with showing his excitement when he makes a good play? And why should he care if the other teams' fans like him?

More important to Barkley is what his opponents think of him. The answer: They may not like him, but they respect him. Three times they have voted him to the all-NBA team. Most say they do not enjoy playing against him because he is so rough.

"He's really hyper, real intense," said Dominique Wilkins of the Atlanta Hawks. "Sometimes his temper really gets him going. You know, he gets a look in his eyes and you know he's ready to play."

Larry Bird says he understands that Barkley's bluster is part of his game. "I'm the type of person who doesn't always

Barkley always shows his true emotions on the court—both the ups and downs.

say the right things myself," Bird said. "But I never apologize for what I've said, even though I may regret them. The best thing you can do is be your own person. And Charles is definitely his own person."

Bird has seen Barkley's antics close up. A few years ago, Bird was on the foul line in the final seconds of a tight Celtics-76ers game at the Philadelphia Spectrum. Even though he is the NBA's best foul shooter, Bird missed the first of two free throws. Barkley, standing nearby, leaned forward and grabbed his throat, giving Bird the "choke" sign. Bird was so rattled that he missed the second shot—allowing the Sixers to win the game.

The truth is Charles Barkley completely changes when the game is over. There is a fire that burns inside him that makes him want to win. But there is also a big heart. Barkley adores those fans who adore him. He spends hours signing autographs or talking about basketball with perfect strangers who approach him in airports or shopping malls.

He also loves to help out kids. Recently, the 76ers got a call from a high school basketball coach in Florida. The coach said he had cut a boy from the team. Now the boy was talking about dropping out of school. Charles Barkley is the boy's hero, the coach said. Would Charles mind talking to the boy for just a few minutes?

The Sixers arranged to have Charles call from their office. But the boy wasn't there. So that night, Charles went home and spent an hour on the phone with the boy. He straightened him out and got him back into the classroom.

"As a person, he's a tremendous human being," said Chuck Person, his old college teammate who now plays for the Indiana Pacers. "He's kind of shy, I guess, laid-back. He's a fun-loving guy. He's dedicated to his family." During

Charles loves meeting his fans, especially children.

games, Person said, Barkley plays like an angry bear. But off the floor, Person calls him a teddy bear.

Certainly he is that way with his family. Barkley's favorite times are when he is alone with his wife, Maureen, and his baby daughter, Christiana. Celebrity life can be exciting, but it can also be tiring. Imagine having people come up to you all day asking for your autograph or wanting to shake your hand. Sometimes it may be fun. But other times you might just want to be left alone with your family.

Charles and his wife were married in 1989. Any new marriage can be stressful, but Barkley's was even more so. He is black, and his wife is white. Every so often when they go out in public together, they hear whispers or see angry stares.

As part of his campaign against drugs, Barkley got to meet First Lady Nancy Reagan in 1987.

At first, that made Barkley angry. Now, he says, he just ignores the people who disapprove.

"For someone to dislike another person because of skin color is silly," he said. "What we're talking about here is pretty simple: It's two people who love each other. Our family and friends understand. I can't worry about pleasing the other people."

And that sums up the straightforward Barkley approach: You can't please everyone, so you have to do what seems right to you.

When people tell him that his interracial marriage can't work, Charles sees that as a challenge. And, remember, Charles Barkley's life has been a series of challenges. He has learned to meet them—and to beat them. It's similar to the time when people told him that he was too short or too fat to make it as a player. He proved them wrong then. He met that challenge.

Now, he says, his biggest challenge is to win the NBA championship.

# Chapter 6

Most NBA players go their whole career without winning a league championship. All-time greats George Gervin, Alex English, and Adrian Dantley each played more than a dozen years—but were never part of a title team. Current all-stars Patrick Ewing, Karl Malone, and Chris Mullin have never even come close. Charles Barkley also falls into this group. And he does not like it.

"Hey, all I want to do is win," he told reporters in 1990. "Anybody who doesn't like it can just get out of the way. I want to win an NBA championship. Not a day goes by that I don't think about it. I'm gonna do it, too. Either that or die trying."

Whether Barkley makes it remains to be seen. The 76ers, who did not make the playoffs in 1987-88, quickly recovered to become one of the better clubs in the NBA. But better isn't good enough. The league has twenty-seven teams, and only one gets to carry home the trophy each year. Since the Sixers won it in 1983, just four teams—the Boston Celtics, Los

Angeles Lakers, Detroit Pistons, and Chicago Bulls—have had a turn winning the championship.

To date, the 1988-89 season was Barkley's favorite. Before that season, Sixers' coach Jimmy Lynam named him the captain of the team. This was added responsibility. Charles would now have to lead not just by scoring points. He would also have to set an example. Early in the season, he did just that. In the final seconds of a game against the Pistons, the Sixers held the slimmest of leads. Coach Lynam described the action: "The clock was running down, we were leading by a point, and a Detroit player took a pass down the lane. Charles was nowhere in sight. The guy laid the ball up and Charles came in and caught the shot. Picked it out of the air. It's like he wills things to happen sometimes. How many players can do that at this level?"

The Sixers climbed back to 46 wins that season, finishing second in their division. Although they were swept from the playoffs by the New York Knicks, there was reason for hope in Philadelphia. Barkley—who had felt all alone since Moses Malone and Julius Erving left—finally had some help. Rookie Hersey Hawkins, a sharp-shooting guard, joined the club. So did forward Ron Anderson, who could join Charles in grabbing rebounds and guarding the other team's best shooter. Center Mike Gminski provided a sweet outside shot. Veteran point guard Maurice Cheeks was still there to direct the offense.

Charles, of course, was the key. He made the All-NBA team for the second straight year. He averaged 25.8 points and 12.5 rebounds per game.

The next season, Barkley hoped, the Sixers could continue climbing the ladder. The club traded Cheeks for talented young point guard Johnny Dawkins. It signed tough power forward Rick Mahorn to help Charles out against

Desire is what made Charles a scoring leader. Here he goes inside against Utah's Mark Eaton, who is nearly a foot taller than Barkley.

body-slamming teams like the Pistons and Bucks. The 76ers wanted to add more good players, but they were stopped by NBA rules. The league has something called the "salary cap." That limits the amount that each team may spend on players. The Sixers were already at the salary cap limit heading into 1989-90. They could spend no more.

How could Charles help? He was already giving 100 percent on the court and, truly, had emerged as one of the three or four best players in the NBA. What more could he do?

Barkley came up with an idea. He offered to take a pay cut. He would give back $250,000 of his $2 million salary if the Sixers would use it to add another good player.

The club was pleased with Barkley's offer, but decided not to take him up on it. Charles was worth the money he was getting, Lynam said. To pay him less would be unfair.

So the 76ers entered the 1989-90 season with their best potential in years, but still missing a few pieces of the puzzle. Barkley was encouraged. He said he was on a mission to prove that he was a winner. The new cast of characters surrounding him would help him achieve his goal. Charles called it, "Put up or shut up time in Philadelphia."

The Sixers put up their best showing since Barkley's rookie season. They won 53 games, lost 29, and took the Atlantic Division title. They went to the second round of the playoffs before losing a heartbreaking seven-game series to the Chicago Bulls. In the final game, Charles and Bulls' star Michael Jordan went head-to-head all night. Each man scored more than 30 points. Each thrilled the crowd with slam dunks and blocked shots. Charles even sunk a three-pointer—a rarity for him.

Barkley was disappointed that the team could not go further. But for him, it had been another great season. In just

The 76ers lost a tough playoff series to the Chicago Bulls in 1990. Here, Charles drives the lane.

his sixth year, he crashed through the 10,000-point and 5,000-rebound barriers for his career. He shot 60 percent from the field for the first time.

Even so, Barkley's scoring average went down for the second straight year. Instead of being upset, he saw this statistic as a positive sign. The team around him was getting better, he said. So the shots could be spread around more. Hawkins and Dawkins were there to help Charles on the offense, and Mahorn and Anderson helped him with the rebounds.

As good a season as it was in Philadelphia, Barkley got some bad news at the end. His shoulder had been sore all season. During the playoffs, the pain became overwhelming. Doctors discovered serious damage to the bone and the ligaments holding his shoulder in place. He needed an operation in the summer.

At first, doctors worried that the surgery might end Charles's career. Even if it didn't, many fans wondered, how much would the injury affect his play? Some believed that a sore shoulder would keep Barkley from making his two favorite moves. One is a quick spin to the baseline after he catches the ball with his back to the basket. The other is a lightning-fast drive down the lane after which he stops on a dime and sinks a six-foot shot—usually while also drawing a foul.

Barkley, too, was worried. It wasn't just his shoulder that was injured. His knees were also hurting. Doctors told him he had the knees of a thirty-seven year-old man. The problem was that he was twenty-seven at the time.

When the 1990-91 season started, it was clear that Charles was hurting. His face would wrinkle in pain while going up to block a shot. Or he would grab his aching shoulder after a rebound. Then he broke the bone in his foot—the injury that almost kept him from the All-Star game. Overall, Charles sat out fifteen games because of injuries and played just a few minutes in several others.

But when he did play, he was as great as usual. The fact that he was able to perform at all with the nagging injuries seems almost a miracle. It makes you wonder if, when he finally retires, Charles's amazing body should be put in the NBA Hall of Fame or sent to a museum for study.

The 1991 NBA All-Star game is just one example. Playing on the broken foot, Barkley won the trophy for best player. For the regular season, he averaged close to 28 points per game, made the All-NBA team, and finished third in the Most Valuable Player voting. And for the second straight year, the

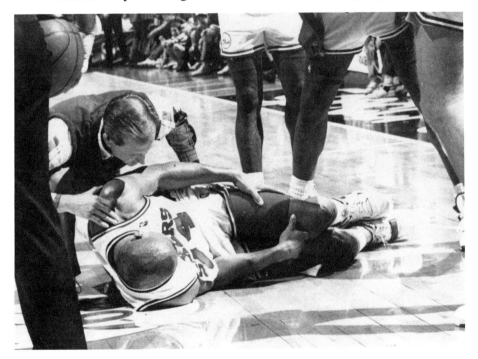

Barkley's bad knees have slowed him down at times.

Sixers won their first-round playoff series, only to get rubbed out by the Chicago Bulls in the second round. The Bulls went on to win the NBA championship.

Once again, Barkley was frustrated by being a great player on a not-so-great team. After just six games, Dawkins tore up his knee and was gone for the season. Mahorn, too, was slowed by injuries. And a trade that sent center Mike Gminski to the Charlotte Hornets for forward Armon Gilliam proved to be a disaster. Sometimes, Charles was so outnumbered by the opposition that he had to feel as if he were on a trampoline while fighting for rebounds.

In his rookie season, Charles got a taste of what it is like to play on a great team. And in the six seasons that followed, he longed to be surrounded again by talented teammates. Finally he got that chance in the summer of 1992—playing on the United States Olympic team.

The Olympic "Dream Team" was the greatest collection of basketball talent ever put together. It included some of Barkley's biggest NBA rivals—Michael Jordan and Patrick Ewing and David Robinson and Karl Malone. The starting power forward was none other than Charles Wade Barkley.

For Charles, making the Dream Team was, indeed, a dream come true. He had tried out for the 1984 team, but was one of the last players cut by coach Bobby Knight. Since then, Barkley wanted to represent his country. He wanted to prove that American players—including himself—are the best in the world.

At the Olympics in Barcelona, Spain, there were no doubts. The Dream Team won all six of its games, some by more than 50 points. Its players seemed like men playing against young boys. Barkley was perhaps its brightest star, leading the team in scoring and finishing second in rebounding. In the end, he proudly wore his gold medal on the plane ride home.

Barkley's home would change before the next season. The Sixers, trying to rebuild their club, traded him to the Phoenix Suns for three players. Suddenly, Barkley was on a new team, playing with new teammates, in a different part of the country. It would be a major adjustment.

But Charles was thrilled. His new club, unlike the Sixers, was full of talent. Forwards Richard Dumas and Tom Chambers helped pull down the rebounds. Guards Kevin Johnson, Danny Ainge, and Dan Majerle scored the baskets and dished the ball off—usually to Barkley. Through most of the 1992–93 season, the Suns had the best record in the NBA. Most experts believed that Charles would be voted the league's most valuable player.

"That would be nice," Barkley said late in the season. "But that's not why I play the game. What I want is to be part of a championship team." The Olympic team, he said, came home a champion, and Charles brought home a medal. But playing in the NBA is tougher than playing against teams from other countries. So he wants the Suns to be champions.

The fans in Phoenix quickly took to Barkley. In a promotion for one game, any fan who shaved his head to look like Barkley got in for free. Hundreds of men—and even a few women—showed up that night with shiny bald heads.

"Words cannot express how happy I feel right now," Barkley said. "This is my best chance to win a championship."

Of course, a few so-called experts said that Charles and the Suns couldn't beat the league's other top teams in the playoffs. Charles doesn't mind their words. In fact he kind of likes to hear them. He loves proving the experts wrong. Over the years, that's been the story of his whole life.

# Career Statistics

## NBA

| Year | Team | GP | FG% | REB | AST | STL | BLK | PTS | AVG |
|---|---|---|---|---|---|---|---|---|---|
| 1984-85 | Philadelphia | 82 | .545 | 703 | 155 | 95 | 80 | 1,148 | 14.0 |
| 1985-86 | Philadelphia | 80 | .572 | 1,026 | 312 | 173 | 125 | 1,603 | 20.0 |
| 1986-87 | Philadelphia | 68 | .594 | 994 | 331 | 119 | 104 | 1,564 | 23.0 |
| 1987-88 | Philadelphia | 80 | .587 | 951 | 254 | 100 | 103 | 2,264 | 28.3 |
| 1988-89 | Philadelphia | 79 | .579 | 986 | 325 | 126 | 67 | 2,037 | 25.8 |
| 1989-90 | Philadelphia | 79 | .600 | 909 | 307 | 148 | 50 | 1,989 | 25.2 |
| 1990-91 | Philadelphia | 67 | .570 | 680 | 284 | 110 | 33 | 1,849 | 27.6 |
| 1991-92 | Philadelphia | 75 | .552 | 830 | 308 | 136 | 44 | 1,730 | 23.1 |
| 1992-93 | Phoenix | 76 | .520 | 928 | 385 | 119 | 74 | 1,944 | 25.6 |
| 1993-94 | Phoenix | 65 | .495 | 727 | 296 | 101 | 37 | 1,402 | 21.6 |
| 1994-95 | Phoenix | 68 | .486 | 756 | 276 | 110 | 45 | 1,561 | 23.0 |
| 1995-96 | Phoenix | 71 | .500 | 821 | 262 | 114 | 56 | 1,649 | 23.2 |
| Total | | 890 | .549 | 10,311 | 3,495 | 1,451 | 818 | 20,740 | 23.3 |

## Where to Write Charles Barkley

Mr. Charles Barkley
c/o Phoenix Suns
P.O. Box 1369
Phoenix, AZ 85001

# Index

Johnson, Kevin, 61
Jones, Bobby, 26, 37
Jordan, Michael, 7, 9, 11, 23,
    39, 43, 56, 60

**K**

Karl, George, 39
Knight, Bobby, 60
Kosky, Dave, 46

**L**

Laimbeer, Bill, 32, 37
Leeds, Alabama, 13, 16, 18, 27
Leeds High School, 18, 19
Listor, Alton, 39
Los Angeles Clippers, 24
Los Angeles Lakers, 24, 53-54
Lynam, Jim, 54, 56

**M**

Mahorn, Rick, 54, 58, 60
Majerle, Dan, 61
Malone, Karl, 53, 60
Malone, Moses, 26, 30, 35,
    37-39, 54
McHale, Kevin, 43
Milwaukee Bucks, 32, 39, 56
Mokeski, Paul, 32, 39
Mullin, Chris, 53

**N**

National Basketball Association
    (NBA), 13, 24, 27, 34,
    56, 60
NBA All-Star Game, 7, 9, 15, 59
NBA commissioner, 45
NBA draft, 23, 24
NBA Hall of Fame, 59
NBA MVP Award, 59

NBA playoffs, 32, 38, 53
New Jersey Nets, 46
New York Knicks, 54

**O**

Olajuwon, Hakeem, 7, 23

**P**

Person, Chuck, 49, 51
Perkins, Sam, 23
Philadelphia 76ers, 7, 9, 11, 13,
    23, 24, 26, 29, 30, 32,
    35-39, 46, 47, 49, 53, 54,
    56, 57, 60, 61
Phoenix Suns, 61
Princeton, N.J., 26

**R**

Robertson, Alvin, 23
Robinson, David, 7, 60
Ruland, Jeff, 37

**S**

Schick Pivotal Player Award, 39
Smith, Sonny, 19-21, 23
Southeast Conference, 21
Stockton, John, 23

**T**

Toney, Andrew, 26, 37, 38
Tuscaloosa, Alabama, 19

**U**

United States Olympic Team,
    60, 61

**W**

Washington Bullets, 32, 37
Wilkins, Dominique, 39, 47
Williams, Pat, 32, 37